Barefoot

Samantha Morrison

Presentation by *BookLeaf Publishing*

Web: www.bookleafpub.com

E-mail: info@bookleafpub.com

ISBN: 9789357213851

First edition 2022

*This collection is dedicated to my parents,
David and Betty.*

ACKNOWLEDGEMENT

Thank you to Andy, James, Richard and Delilah for your patience while I dedicated so much time to this project. Thank you to Kayla for being my beta reader and offering your insight. You all are deeply loved and appreciated.

Barefoot

The soles of my feet
are imprinted with
the memories of my youth.
Every blade of grass
that nestled between my toes,
every mile I ran,
every tree I climbed,
every piece of gravel
kicked out of the way,
every bale of hay I
mounted like stairs,
every mud puddle
I jumped in,
splashing rain water
all over clean church clothes,
every time I hopped, skipped and jumped
over hot black asphalt.
All of these memories
now protected
every time I put on my shoes.

Brave Bastard

She stood on her own.

He didn't mean to leave her so soon.

I am one.

Winter

Bound by frozen truth;
death will take its toll
on unsuspecting life.
Death,
hidden by a blanket of white;
so delicate,
so soft.
Deceiving the rest
of what lies beneath
the bellowing folds.

False Memory

A trailer is engulfed
in flames.
The fire hot on my face
as I peek over my
mother's protective shoulder.
My aunt is
talking to my dad.
My cousins are nestled
behind the barrier
the adults have created
to shield them
from the ghastly scene.
I can hear the sirens
on their way to help.
Red and blue
lights imprint
on my brain,
blending to an awful
shade of purple.
This is how I remember it;
only, it never really happened.

Cheeseburgers at Midnight

Dad and I
always had insomnia
on the same nights.
Or, rather,
he had insomnia;
I just woke up
in the middle of the night sometimes.
My bare feet would pad across the linoleum
as I rubbed the sleep from my eyes.
He's pick me up,
sit me on the counter.
He'd cook the burgers.
I'd add the cheese;
careful not to burn my fingers
in the hot grease.
Simply assembled with
bread for buns,
ketchup and mustard.
He'd tell me jokes
and I'd giggle
in between bites,
until crusts were all
that remained.
Then, he'd guide me back to bed,
tucking me in tight

and I'd go to sleep.
I always thought that
he went to bed, too,
but I imagine he stayed awake.

Wood Stove

Fed with wood
chopped under winter snow.
A healthy flame
send embers afloat
up the chimney
illuminating a gray sky.
A pot belly
that is never really full.

Tree

Winter burnt
bark peeling back
a banana peel in the spring sun.
Swaying from top to bottom;
creaking, moaning;
filling the air with sadness.
Limbs outstretched
to hold itself up
from falling to its demise.

Little Grandma

sat at
the end of the bed,
rocking my foot
back and forth,
like she had
so many times before.
"It will be okay,"
she said.
I awoke
when the phone rang.

That Old House

The paint was peeling;
the siding cracked with age.
Windows boarded up,
fighting off the cold.
Toys are in the yard
and cars sit upon blocks.
The grass is brown
from losing its life to winter.
Stains from weather
leave tear streaks
down the front of that old house;
the one that I called
Home.

(Fear) the Reaper

-a nightmare-

Little girl in a yellow dress;
her hair in dark braids;
sits in a smoke-filled bar
watching her ballerina dance
to music unheard.
Men all around her
yell and curse
above the sound
from the speakers.
Newscasters on the t.v.
broadcasting amongst the trees.
A soldier beside her
screams
at something they say.
His anger vibrates
so violently
she can feel it
deep in her chest.
She's scared and starts to cray
and he tries to comfort her.
A tank smashes
the bricks to dust
and the ballerina

stops dancing
but the song
keeps playing.

Hitchcock

Held my hand,
leading me through
the dark maze of the macabre.
Introduced me
to the evil psyches
that exist in the human mind.
Preparing me
for the hard truth
I would need later in life.
Hitchcock stole
my innocence
and I don't want it back.

Boy Crazy

Allen,
who asked me
if I would go with him.
To which I responded,
"Where?"

Gates.
He was cruel to me
and I couldn't
spell his last name,
but I still liked him.

Danny,
who I like,
but
he went out
with my cousin instead.

Craig…
I was 12.
He was 18.
Don't judge me…
it was a crush.

Justin,

who I liked…
until he felt up my flat chest,
and
I had to kick him in the balls.

Then there was
Russell.
My first boyfriend.
My first dance.
My first kiss.
My first broken heart.

My favorite

time of day is right before
the sun sets
behind the horizon.
Before the world
is engulfed in darkness;
when the clouds disappear
leaving the sky orange,
streaked with blue and pink,
as if God were the artist
and the sky His canvas,
creating His masterpiece
before our very eyes.

Rumors

When I was a little girl,
I overheard the grown-ups talking…

"I think she started the fire."
"He used to hit her.
And she was only 14
when they got married."
"Maybe she was finally sick
of his shit."

"He can't be his son.
I mean, look at him. He looks just like
you-know-who.
They're not fooling anyone."

"You know he killed
a guy, right?
Beat him to death with his bare hands."

"Did you see the paper?
Another lawyer quit
under mysterious circumstances."
"What do you think they will do with the
crossbows they used?"

"She's already got a new boyfriend.
Why doesn't he just
give her the divorce?"

"The gun they used…they stole it from me."

"Can you believe she said that
about him? He would never
do something like that
to a girl like her."

When I was a little girl,
I overheard the grown-ups
talking.

Esther

I don't know
that she ever
addressed me directly,
but I remember
her voice;
a soft, calming tone;
an accent on her lips
from a state down south.
I went to an auction once,
on her farm,
and while strange hands
rummaged
through her things,
an auctioneer spewed out bids:
higher,
lower.
My slightly overstuffed relative
sat on a white rusted patio chair,
fanning herself.
My aunt braided
her long gray hair.
Effortlessly,
she twisted the strands of silver straw
and pinned it down
on top of her head.

Lucifer

was an albino rat,
with fire-red eyes
and a long gray tail.
Every morning
he greeted me with a kiss,
and when I wasn't
at school,
we shared our meals.
We enjoyed
long walks together,
and when he grew tired,
I'd carry him on my shoulder.
During the winter,
he took naps in my hair.

(The) Sunflower

Majestic and regal
head held high
standing far above
the rest.
Soaking up the sun's warmth
following the star's movement,
east to west
across the clear blue sky.

Jumper

Hot shingles scratched
our bare feet and seared
our soles as we lugged the
pillows out the window.

     Peering over the edge,
we tossed the safe landing
down to burnt summer grass,
bickering to each other

     about who would go first.
Because I was the oldest,
I went and it seemed so
high up that when

     my toes were close to the gutter,
I considered running back and
through the open window. Instead,
I jumped.

     Hot shingles scratched
our bare feet and seared
our soles as we lugged the
pillows out the window.

Autumn

A cool, crisp chill
cascades from the peaks
high atop a hill.

Leaves will soon change.
Colors quickly fade
from orange to brown.

Snow will follow
with blankets of white,
leaving life hollow.

Classic

Lovers gaze into each
others' eyes
under a soft filtered lens.
An unrealistic
representation
of what love looks like.
Ironic,
to be in black and white,
when love
is definitively not.

Night and Day

He
prepared me
for my future life.

She
prepared my soul
for the after life.